Compton Castle

Devon

THE NATIONAL TRUST

Above Sir Humphrey Gilbert

Right The armillary sphere
was set up in the Rose
Garden in 1983 to
commemorate the 400th
anniversary of Sir Humphrey
Gilbert's colonisation of
Newfoundland

LIVING AT COMPTON CASTLE

BY GEOFFREY GILBERT

My ancestor Geoffrey Gilbert came here from Totnes around 1329, the year he married Joan de Compton, the heiress to the property, which at that stage was probably a manor house. The family have lived here ever since, with a gap of 146 years between 1785, when they sold it to James Templer of Stover near Newton Abbot, and 1931, when my father, Commander Walter Raleigh Gilbert, managed to buy back the castle and surrounding orchard.

I was born just before the Second World War. I remember the peacocks roosting in the west wing, and my brother Raleigh and I throwing stones up to the doorways in the towers. I also remember the Home Guard practising their fire drill, and my parents ploughing up what is now the car-park for the 'Dig for Victory' food campaign. My half-brother Humphrey was a Spitfire pilot in the Battle of Britain, and Raleigh later became a well-known racing commentator.

My parents did an enormous amount of work carefully restoring the castle room by room before deciding to give it to the National Trust in 1951. After that, they set about rebuilding the Great Hall, restoring the west wing and constructing the Rose Garden. After we came to live here in 1984 with our children Humphrey, Arabella and Walter, my wife Angela introduced a flock of Jacob sheep and subsequently raised money for the second pergola and the Knot Garden.

Historically, my family's greatest claim to fame is its involvement in the early attempts to colonise the New World. Sir Humphrey Gilbert's colonisation of Newfoundland in 1583 founded the British Empire. He was followed by his half-brother, Sir Walter Raleigh, who took up the challenge and organised the Roanoke colony on the Outer Banks of North Carolina in 1585. Sir Humphrey's son Raleigh Gilbert sailed to what is now Maine and set up Fort St George in 1607.

We hope you enjoy your visit to our home and will find it interesting.

Top Commander Walter Raleigh Gilbert, who bought back Compton Castle in 1931 and rebuilt the Great Hall. Portrait by Denis Fildes in the Solar

Above Geoffrey and Angela Gilbert

TOUR OF THE CASTLE

'The approach is unforgettable.' NIKOLAUS PEVSNER

The Entrance Front

The towering North Front was fortified
to protect Compton against French raids.

In the centre is the main portcullis
entrance, which is flanked by projections
with 'machicolations' – holes through which
missiles could be dropped on an attacker
below. Behind this central screen is an open
courtyard which leads to the Great Hall.
Set back beyond the tower to the left is
a secondary portcullis gateway, which is
defended in the same way. The large pointed
window on the right lights the Chapel. Stout
iron bars protect this potentially vulnerable
point in the castle's defences. At ground level,
loopholes and lookouts allowed the defenders
to observe and fire on any hostile approach.

Although the castle fell partially into ruin
in the 19th century, its walls have survived in
very good condition. They were built of local
limestone a metre thick, with red sandstone
and white Beer stone dressings, and granite
corbels and lintels for the machicolations.

Key dates

1340s Geoffrey Gilbert builds the core of the
present house

c.1450–75 Manor house enlarged

1520s North Front defences and curtain wall
added as a protection against threat of French
raiding parties

1955 Great Hall rebuilt

Top The Entrance Front

Above Border in the Rose
Garden

Right Seat by the Lily Pond

*Turn right out of the Inner Couryard and go through the door
up the steps to the Rose Garden.*

The Rose Garden

The Rose Garden was created in the 1950s.
The armillary sphere on a granite plinth
was forged in 1983 to commemorate the
400th anniversary of the colonisation of
Newfoundland by Sir Humphrey Gilbert.
A rose plan is available at reception.

The Knot Garden

Next to the Rose Garden is a knot garden,
created in medieval style in 2003. It was
funded entirely from public donations and
events at the property, as was the right-hand
side of the pergola, which was added in 2001.

*Return past the main entrance and walk through the gateway
on the far right to view the west wing.*

Above The North Front features several projecting machicolations, through which missiles could be dropped on an attacker

Left The large traceried window of the Chapel was a vulnerable point in the castle's defences and so was protected with a stout metal grille

The Inner Court

You enter an inner courtyard, which is enclosed by the 7.3-metre-high defensive wall that surrounds three sides of the castle. It also acts as a retaining wall, with buttresses holding back the higher ground to the west. Look out for the 'putlog' holes in the curtain wall, in which the original builders' scaffolding would have been fixed.

Walk round to the steps at the far (south) end of the courtyard.

From this position, you can get a good view of the back of the Great Hall (in the centre with large pointed windows and massive Delabole slate roof). This was carefully reconstructed in 1955 following its mid-14th-century form. The windows were plotted out from surviving fragments of the originals, which had been reassembled and measured. They were made from Oxfordshire greenstone, which very closely resembles the stone originally used.

To your right is the watchtower built in the south-east corner of the court wall and provided with many small windows and loopholes.

Walk towards the Great Hall and turn right to enter the Old Kitchen.

The Old Kitchen

This imposing space with its solid barrel-vaulted ceiling was built about 1520, and has changed little since then, apart from the wall opposite the fireplace, which was rebuilt in the 17th century. The kitchen was placed away from the main building as a precaution against fire. The high windows would have let out any heat and smoke that did not go up the chimney.

The huge *fireplace* fills the entire east wall and has three flues, with bread ovens on either side, which were heated independently of the roasting hearth. When the food was ready, it was dispatched through the serving hatch by the door to a servant, who would have to carry it across the open courtyard to the Great Hall.

The *ironwork* in the fireplace was largely collected by John Seymour Lindsay (see p.8), who bequeathed it to Commander Gilbert in his will.

Walk through the narrow angled passage on the right.

The Scullery

This occupies the ground floor of one of the inner towers, provided with two loopholes for close-range defence of the outer walls nearby. It was probably used as a scullery – hence the drain in the floor, through which waste water could be slopped out.

Walk up the spiral staircase. Watch out for the low doorway and uneven steps. The small, heavily barred room on the floor above possibly served as a guardroom. Return to the Old Kitchen and walk across the inner court to reach the Great Hall.

The oak door in the passage outside the Old Kitchen was removed from one of the bedrooms and is probably 500 years old.

Top The inner Court, with the rebuilt Great Hall on the left and the south-east tower on the right

Above The narrow Scullery windows reveal the thickness of the castle walls

Opposite The Kitchen

7

MODEL
On the medieval-style long table in the centre of the room is a model of Sir Humphrey Gilbert's vessel, the *Squirrel*, in which he lost his life on 9 September 1583, when she foundered in a storm off the Azores on the way home from Newfoundland.

Opposite **The Great Hall**

The Screens Passage
The *bronze badge* was given to Commander Gilbert by the officers of HMS *Squirrel*, the twelfth of this name in the Royal Navy since Sir Humphrey Gilbert's *Squirrel*.

Pass through the screen on the left to reach the Great Hall.

The Great Hall
This was a roofless ruin until 1955, when Commander Gilbert rebuilt it in its original form with an oak arch-braced roof. The *oak screen* and the *panelling* at the far end of the room are based on Elizabethan panelling from a house near Exeter (now in the Victoria & Albert Museum in London).

Furnishings
For his new Great Hall, Commander Gilbert preferred to commission good modern reproductions of the best traditional pieces that would age with the panelling, rather than buy dubious dark oak 'antiques'. So the *tables* were reduced copies of rare medieval examples in the Great Hall at Penshurst in Kent. The *sofas* round the fire were inspired by a famous prototype of the 1660s at Knole in Kent.

The *wooden hanging light* is an interesting 1950s re-interpretation of medieval forms for modern needs. It was designed by J. Seymour Lindsay, an expert on early metal-work who designed all the iron latches and handles around the house. Lindsay did much work for Lutyens and was responsible in 1946 for the silver altar rails and altar plate of the Battle of Britain memorial chapel in Westminster Abbey.

Pictures
Three family portraits hang on the far wall. On the left-hand side is *Sir Humphrey Gilbert*, who colonised Newfoundland in 1583. The picture is inscribed with his motto *Quid non* ('Why not?') – the rallying cry of explorers from his day to this.

The centre portrait is of Sir Humphrey's younger son *Raleigh Gilbert*, who led the attempt to found a colony in Maine in 1607. He was also involved in establishing the first permanent European settlement in North America at Jamestown, Virginia.

The right-hand portrait is of Sir Humphrey's eldest son *Sir John Gilbert II*, who accompanied his uncle Sir Walter Raleigh to Guiana in 1595 and to the sacking of Cadiz the following year.

Heraldry
The *framed heraldic chart* near the entrance shows the quarterings of the Gilbert family and explains the *shields of arms* around the Great Hall. On the screen below the Minstrels' Gallery hangs the coat of arms of the de Compton family (containing three shoveller ducks), who held these lands for seven generations before 1329.

Photographs and stamps
On the far left-hand wall is a labelled display of photographs and stamps commemorating the exploits of the Gilbert family as pioneering explorers of the New World.

Go through the door in the far left corner to reach the Sub-Solar.

The Sub-Solar

This room was originally used as a cellar. Around 1450–75, the whole of the block to the west of the Great Hall was rebuilt to provide more spacious family quarters. Here the ceiling was raised to make a new withdrawing room.

Furnishings

The chest on the right as you entered the room belonged to *General Sir Walter Raleigh Gilbert* (1785–1853). A mezzotint of 1852 after his portrait hangs to the right of the chest. At 63 years old, and on horseback, he led the brigade which won the battle of Gujarat in India in 1849. He also won several racing trophies, notably at Plymouth and Cheltenham; and was awarded a medal for rescuing a man from a lake in Cheltenham whilst still booted and spurred.

The portrait above the chest is of *Captain Charles Colt*, who was General Gilbert's aide-de-camp and married one of his daughters in India.

The *dummy boards*, on the left, are Flemish. They were given to Mrs Geoffrey Gilbert by her aunt and uncle, Mr and Mrs Anthony Post. They had been passed down through the Post family for several generations.

Climb the 15th-century stone spiral staircase to reach the Solar.

The Solar

The Solar was the main private living room in large medieval houses, and was usually placed, as here, on the first floor above the high end of the Great Hall.

On your left, you may peep into an ante-chamber, now used as a study. The modern oak staircase at the far end of the room has the Gilbert squirrel carved on the newel post. The *fireplace* was reduced in size in the 15th century, when the withdrawing room below was heightened.

Furnishings

The *child's rocking chair* was given to Raleigh Gilbert (1936–98) by his godmother. The *two tapestry chairs* were worked by General Gilbert's wife while her husband was on frequent trips to India.

Pictures

The *two large portraits* are of *Commander Walter Raleigh Gilbert* and his wife *Joan*, both painted by Denis Fildes. The *watercolour studies of camellias* are by Mrs Joan Gilbert, who painted flowers growing within the castle walls. Above the window looking into the Chapel on the far wall is a copy made in 1768 of Thomas Gainsborough's portrait of *Anne Bennet of Hexworthy* in Cornwall.

Flanking the fireplace are three 17th-century portraits of members of the *Fairfax family*, which came from the Gilberts' previous home, The Priory in Bodmin. These may be of Thomas Fairfax (1584–1648) of Civil War fame, with his wife, Anne Vere, and their daughter Mary.

Go down to the Great Hall and out to the front court, from which you can enter the Chapel.

Above **The squirrel finial on the Solar stairs is taken from the Gilbert family coat of arms**

Opposite **The Solar**

The Chapel

The doorway appears to date from the first building phase of the 1340s, but this wing was completely remodelled in the mid-15th century at the same time as the adjoining Solar block. The Perpendicular-style windows certainly date from around 1450, and the interior also shows signs of alteration. Opposite the altar are *two small squints* at ground level and a *window* above, through which the mass could be observed from the Sub-Solar and the Solar. To the right of the altar is a small *basin* within a trefoil-headed niche known as a piscina, into which was emptied water used for washing communion vessels.

The Chapel was refurnished in the 20th century and remains in use. All the children of the current Gilbert family were baptised here.

Furnishings

The *modern pews* bear the arms of the de Comptons (*sable, a chevron ermine between three shoveller ducks argent*); the Gilberts (*argent, on a chevron sable, three roses argent*); and the Willocks (the family of Commander Gilbert's wife Joan). All three are decorated with a squirrel in allusion to the Gilberts' crest.

The *altar table* and *hanging light* were designed by J. Seymour Lindsay. The *priest's folding chair* was originally used by the Rev. W. R. Gilbert while a naval chaplain in the 1870s. The *tapestry stool* was worked by Captain Gilbert Roberts, RN, a relation of the Gilberts who was appointed by Churchill to develop anti-U-boat tactics for the North Atlantic convoys in the Second World War.

Brass rubbings

The framed rubbings are from the ancient brasses in Otterden church, Kent, commemorating the *Aucher* grandfather and great-grandfather of Sir Humphrey Gilbert's wife. Their arms were *ermine, in chief azure, three lions rampart or*.

The rubbing of the ledger slab of *Ager Gilbert*, son of Raleigh Gilbert, in Marldon church dated 1661, shows his arms impaled with that of his wife Margaret, daughter of John Walrond of Bovey: *argent, three bulls' heads sable*. He was the great-nephew of Sir Walter Raleigh.

Left The Perpendicular
windows in the Chapel date
from the mid-15th century

Opposite The altar

13

In 1394 William Gilbert was
given a licence 'to receive
in his ship called the *Charity*
in the Port of Dartmouth,
100 pilgrims and ship them
to Santiago [de Compostela
in northern Spain] to pay
their vows and bring them
back to England'.

Right The tomb of John
Gilbert and his wife
Elizabeth in Exeter
Cathedral (before
restoration)

Opposite above The west
end of the castle was rebuilt
by Otho Gilbert I in the
mid-15th century. His son
John added the surrounding
wall (on the left)

Opposite below Effigy
in plate armour on the
cenotaph commemorating
Otho Gilbert I in Marldon
church

COMPTON CASTLE AND THE GILBERTS

THE DE COMPTON FAMILY

The Compton lands belonged to the bishops of Exeter until 1138, when they were granted to Aluric de Compton and his descendants. Seven generations of the de Compton family were to live here over the next two centuries.

Geoffrey Gilbert (d.1349)

Compton had passed out of the hands of the de Comptons by 1329, when the co-heiress to the estate, Joan de Compton, married Geoffrey Gilbert, who came from Totnes at the head of the Dart, the river that was to play such a large part in the story of the Gilbert family. He had been elected MP for the town in 1326, and as the King's representative in the area he had the unpopular task of collecting unpaid taxes required to finance the wars against the Scots. He also administered justice to those convicted of piracy on the high seas – a constant problem in those lawless times.

Geoffrey Gilbert translated his wealth into stone, enlarging the old building into a manor house which forms the core of the present castle. In 1343 he funded a chantry chapel in the church of the Trinitarian Friars at Totnes, where prayers would be said for the repose of his soul after death. Only six years later, he was dead, and the first prayers were being chanted.

Otho Gilbert I (1417–94)

In the 1460s Geoffrey Gilbert's great-grandson Otho provided West Country ships to fight the French, who continued to threaten the south coasts of Devon and Cornwall. His loyal service to the Crown was recognised in 1475, when he was appointed Sheriff of Devon.

Between around 1450 and 1475, he rebuilt and extended the west end of the castle, which contained the family quarters, and improved the Chapel. He was buried in nearby Marldon church, which he partly rebuilt and where he is commemorated by a handsome canopied tomb.

Otho's son, John (d.1539), succeeded to the estate in 1494 and around 1520 made the final major changes to the house. He added the impressive battlemented front with its two portcullis entrances, surrounding the whole with a high curtain wall. Compton was close enough to the sea to be vulnerable to marauding French ships, and these fortifications were probably designed to protect against them.

John Gilbert married Elizabeth Croker, but they had no children, and so in 1539 Compton passed to their nephew, also christened Otho. Otho Gilbert II had been brought up at Greenway, a Gilbert property on the Dart (now also in the care of the National Trust). In 1531 he had married Katherine Champernowne – an alliance that transformed the Gilbert fortunes.

The band of brothers

Katherine came from another influential south Devon family, the Champernownes of Modbury. Her brother, Sir Arthur, was Vice-Admiral of Devon. Her aunt, Kat Astley, taught Princess Elizabeth to read and was to remain a trusted lady-in-waiting at the Queen's court. By Otho, Katherine had three sons: Sir John, Sir Humphrey and Adrian. After Otho's early death in 1547, she married Walter Raleigh of Hayes Barton and bore him two sons, Sir Carew and Sir Walter. Proud, ambitious, short-tempered and fearless, these five brothers formed a close-knit band that left its mark not only on the county and the country, but also on a distant continent – America.

Sir John Gilbert I (1533–96)
Defeating the Armada

Otho Gilbert's eldest son John inherited Compton in 1547. The castle stands only three miles from the inviting anchorage at Torbay and so would have been in the front line of any Spanish invasion. As Vice-Admiral of Devon, he played a leading part in marshalling ships, seamen and supplies to meet the threat of the Spanish Armada in 1588. Dartmouth – second only to Plymouth among the West Country ports – provided the *Crescent* and the *Harte* for the English fleet, while Sir John himself supplied the 150-ton *Gabriel*. His brothers Adrian Gilbert and Sir Walter Raleigh sponsored the *Elizabeth* and the 300-ton *Roebuck*, which was the largest and best-known. The commanders of the English fleet, Sir Francis Drake and Sir John Hawkins, were both Devon men, and their comprehensive defeat of the Spanish Armada marked one of the proudest moments in Devon's long maritime history.

One of the first and greatest prizes of the sea-battle was the Spanish galleon *Nuestra Señora del Rosario*, which surrendered to Drake on 1 August 1588. Her early capture boosted English morale and helped to tip the balance decisively against the Spanish. The vessel was towed into Torbay, and then to the safer harbour of Dartmouth, where she became the responsibility of Sir John Gilbert, as Deputy Lieutenant of Devon. Gilbert organised a careful inventory of the ship's armaments and stores, which provided an invaluable insight into Spanish battle tactics. The crew were kept prisoner in the old barn at Torre Abbey (known ever since as the Spanish Barn) before being moved to near Greenway, where Sir John put them to work building walls.

Opposite Queen Elizabeth I, who supported the Gilbert family's American expeditions provided she did not have to contribute financially

Below The Spanish Armada in crescent formation retreats to the right. Detached from the main body of the fleet in the left foreground, the Spanish galleon *Nuestra Señora del Rosario* is about to surrender to Sir Francis Drake

A PRESENT FOR THE QUEEN

In April 1596 Sir John Gilbert presented Queen Elizabeth with a parrot, which his nephew Sir John Gilbert II had presumably brought back from Guiana (see p.22): *I have sent this bearer, my servant, of purpose unto you with the parakito, and have given him a great charge for the carrying of him. He will eat all kinds of meat and nothing will hurt him except it be very salt. If you put him on the table at meal time he will make choice of his meat. He must be kept very warm, and after he hath filled himself he will set in a gentlewoman's ruff all the day. In the afternoon he will eat bread or oatmeal groats, drink water or claret wine; every night he is put in the cage and covered warm. My servant more at large will tell you all his conditions and qualities. Surely if he be well taught he will speak anything.*

Sir Humphrey Gilbert (1539–83)
Pioneer of the West

Otho Gilbert's second son, Humphrey, was born on the family estate at Greenway and educated at Eton and Oxford. As a boy, he was introduced to the court of the young Princess Elizabeth by his great-aunt Kate Astley. Elizabeth was fond of Humphrey and his brothers, but was reluctant to support their ambitious (and expensive) schemes.

In 1562 Humphrey joined the English garrison defending the fortress of Le Havre from its French attackers. He fought bravely and was wounded, but survived, unlike much of the English force, which succumbed to disease in this disastrous campaign. He was described as 'of higher stature than … the common sort, and of complexion cholerike'.

Like many of his contemporaries, Humphrey Gilbert dreamt of finding a western sea route to China round the northern tip of America. (The Spanish and Portuguese already controlled the southern routes.) In 1566 he drew up *A Discourse of a Discoverie for a new Passage to Cataia* (i.e. China). Addressed to his brother, Sir John Gilbert, it argued that a passage existed 'North-west from us through a sea that lieth on the northside of Labrador'.

From 1566 Humphrey Gilbert found himself serving closer to home, in Sir Henry Sidney's bitter campaign to pacify Ireland. As colonel-in-chief of Munster, he put down a rebellion in the county with ruthless efficiency. He was knighted for his services in 1570. Like many who tried to 'plant' loyal Protestant colonies in Ireland, Gilbert was already looking further west for more peaceful territories to colonise in America.

In June 1578 the Queen granted Sir Humphrey a six-year licence:

> to discover, search, find out and view such remote heathen and barbarous lands, countries and territories, not actually possessed of any Christian prince or people, as to him, his heirs and assigns … shall seem good, and the same to have, hold, occupy and enjoy to him, his heirs and assigns forever.

In effect, this meant the eastern seaboard of North America to the north of Florida, which the Spanish had already begun to colonise, as the ever-cautious Queen was loath to antagonise Spain. Sir Humphrey sunk all his resources into this expensive project, which entailed assembling a fleet of seven ships at Dartmouth. It included, as flagship, the *Anne Ager* (named after his wife), the tiny *Squirrel* (named after the Gilbert crest), and the *Falcon* and the *Hope of Greenway*, which were commanded by his half-brothers, Walter and Carew Raleigh, respectively. They set sail on 26 September 1578, which was late in the season, and, perhaps not surprisingly, were driven back by bad weather. Walter Raleigh was the only one to get out of coastal waters, but by the time he reached the Azores, food was running low, and the crew, many of whom were little better than pirates, mutinied. Raleigh was forced to turn back, his ship 'sore battered and disabled'.

Although this first expedition was a financial disaster, Sir Humphrey was undaunted. In 1580 he commissioned a Portuguese pilot, Simon Fernandez, to reconnoitre the North American coastline

A SCHOOL FOR SEAMEN
In 1573 Sir Humphrey urged the Queen to found a new university in London. Queen Elizabeth's Academy would instruct the sons of the nobility and gentry in the skills of map-making, navigation and astronomy that were vital in the new Age of Exploration. History was ransacked for heroes – role-models who could inspire the next generation of seamen. Sir Humphrey also hoped to raise the status of seafaring, which many still equated with piracy. The Queen turned down his farsighted scheme because of the cost.

looking for a suitable site for a new colony.

To finance a second expedition, Gilbert offered sponsors vast stakes in the new continent: no fewer than three million acres were promised to the poet Sir Philip Sidney. Royal support was vital, but the Queen was at first lukewarm, marking Gilbert down as 'a man noted of not good hap [luck] by sea.' However, Walter Raleigh managed to change her mind, so much so that she sent Gilbert 'a very excellent Jewell … an anckor of gold set with 29 diamondes with the portracture of a Queene'.

On 11 June 1583, Gilbert set sail from Plymouth in his flagship, the *Delight*. Raleigh followed in the *Barke Raleigh*, but turned back after only two days, pleading disease and shortage of victuals. Their destination was Newfoundland, which was already well known to Dartmouth fishermen for the richness of its fishing grounds. On 3 August Gilbert landed at St John's, which he promptly claimed for England. He was delighted with what he found: '… a very rich domain, the Country being very good and full of all sorts of victual as fish, both of the fresh water and sea-fish, deer, pheasants, partridges, swans and divers fowles else.' Many of his crew were less impressed, having been lured to America by the prospect of Spanish gold, not Canadian cod. Gilbert was obliged to sail south, but on 29 August disaster struck. The *Delight*, the largest ship in his fleet, ran aground and was wrecked. 80 crew drowned, and mineral samples and other vital records of this new land were lost. In despair, Gilbert turned for home. He now had only two vessels left: the tiny *Squirrel* and the *Golden*

Hind. Gilbert, however, was determined to make the Atlantic crossing in the *Squirrel*, despite its fragility: 'I will not forsake my little Company going homeward, with whom I have passed so many storms and perils.' The voyage went well until they reached the Azores, where a storm blew up. Edward Hayes in the *Golden Hind* watched the disaster unfold:

> In the afternoon the frigate [*Squirrel*] was near cast away, oppressed by waves, yet at that time recovered; and giving forth signs of joy, the General sitting abaft with a book in his hand, cried unto us in the *Hinde* (so often as we did approach within hearing), 'We are as near to heaven by sea as by land.'

At midnight the *Squirrel*'s lights suddenly disappeared. 'In that moment the frigate was devoured and swallowed up of the sea', and Gilbert and his crew were drowned.

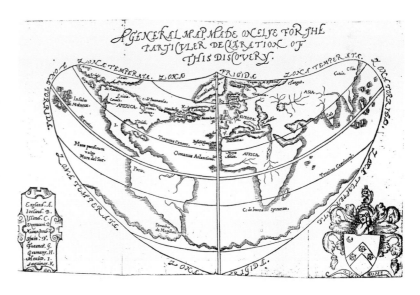

Adrian Gilbert (c.1541–1628)

Sir Humphrey's younger brother shared his fascination with exploration, and in 1584 Adrian Gilbert renewed his royal licence to hunt for the North-West Passage. He owned the 70-ton *Elizabeth* and supplied a vessel to Walter Raleigh's 1591–2 expedition to Panama, but preferred to remain on dry land. He settled a mile up the Dart from Greenway at Sandridge, which he inherited through his wife, Elinor Fulford, and his close friend and neighbour, the explorer John Davis. For 30 years he worked closely with his half-brother Walter, who appointed him surveyor for the rebuilding of Sherborne Castle in Dorset in 1593. Adrian Gilbert also redesigned the Sherborne gardens, successfully introducing exotics brought back from the New World. The result so impressed Sir Robert Cecil that he asked Gilbert to design a water feature for his own vast formal garden at Theobalds in Hertfordshire. Adrian Gilbert also indulged in astrology and assisted Mary, Countess of Pembroke with her alchemical experiments.

Sir Walter Raleigh (1554–1618)

The Roanoke Island colony in North Carolina

Raleigh first caught the exploring bug while reading in his half-brother Humphrey's library at Limehouse in east London. He turned his own Thames-side home, Durham House, into the intellectual crucible of the new Age of Exploration, bringing together there such visionaries as the astrologer John Dee and the mathematician Thomas Harriot.

In March 1584 Raleigh persuaded the Queen to let him renew Sir Humphrey's licence to explore and colonise America. A first reconnoitring voyage later that year to Roanoke Island off the coast of North Carolina proved very promising: 'We found the people most gentle, loving and faithful, void of all guile and treason, and such as lived after the manner of the Golden Age.' Raleigh was encouraged to finance a new colonising expedition. The Queen refused to let him sail with it, so he turned – almost inevitably – to a Devon cousin, Sir Richard Grenville, to command the fleet, which sailed from Plymouth in 1585. The colonists reached Roanoke in August, where they built Fort Raleigh and christened the territory Virginia in honour of the Virgin Queen. The initial mood of optimism soon evaporated. Winter was fast approaching, and it was vital that crops were planted, but the seeds they had brought with them had been spoiled on the journey, and most of the colonists were

Below The North Carolina coastline, showing Roanoke Island in the centre left, where Raleigh's first colony was established. Engraving from Theodor de Bry's *America*, 1590

soldiers, not farmers. So they became dependent for food on the natives, who grew increasingly suspicious as more and more of their number were struck down by European diseases. Suspicion turned to violence, climaxing in the murder of the native chieftain Wingina in a bloody skirmish.

Among the party was the artist John White, who mapped the territory and painted careful watercolours of the local people and the flora and fauna. Alas, much of this invaluable material was lost in 1586, when the colonists abandoned Roanoke and returned home.

Despite this setback, Raleigh refused to give up his dream of an American colony. In May 1587 a second party of colonists set sail, led by John White. They returned to Roanoke, where they discovered to their horror that the fifteen remaining members of the first colony had been killed. White repaired the devastated encampment, and rejoiced at the birth of a granddaughter, who was christened Virginia – the first child of English parents to be born in North America. But White proved a poor leader, whom the colonists gradually turned against, forcing him to sail back to England. He promised to return with fresh supplies, but the Spanish Armada intervened, and he was not able to fulfil his promise until 1590. He found the Roanoke settlement deserted and overgrown; but carved into a post was the word 'CROATOAN', a nearby Indian settlement, which seemed to indicate that the colonists had abandoned Roanoke in good order and moved there. But bad weather prevented White from confirming this. He returned to England, consigning his granddaughter and the other vanished colonists 'to the merciful help of the Almighty'.

Raleigh had been one of Elizabeth's most favoured courtiers, but he was deeply distrusted by her successor, James I, who had him convicted of treason and imprisoned in the Tower. When Raleigh was finally executed in 1618, he laid his head on the block facing west, towards the land that had inspired his dreams.

THE LOST COLONY
With the passing years, the mystery of the 'Lost Colony' grew, until 1701, when an expedition to Croatoan Island came on a party of unusually pale-skinned Indians with grey eyes and brown hair, who spoke and read English. Could these be the descendants of the colonists, who, abandoning hope of help from home, had made their peace with the local population and gradually been absorbed into it?

Top Sir Walter Raleigh about 1585; miniature by Nicholas Hilliard

Left A typically precise watercolour by John White of one of the Algonquian tribesmen he encountered

21

Sir John Gilbert II (1575–1608)

Sir Humphrey's eldest son, John, accompanied his uncle, Walter Raleigh, on his voyage to Guiana in 1595. They journeyed up the Orinoco river in search of El Dorado, the legendary 'Golden Man', who was said to bathe in gold every day. The expedition was yet another disaster, yielding only some rock samples, which turned out to be fool's gold.

It did, however, encourage Raleigh to write *The Discovery of the Large, Rich and Beautiful Empire of Guiana*, one of the first great works of travel literature. Queen Elizabeth was unconvinced by his arguments for colonisation, but in the long term it was to provide a very influential template for the British Empire. John Gilbert also served with his uncle in the 1596 attack on Cadiz,

during which a second Spanish armada was destroyed. Gilbert was knighted for his brave conduct in the battle. He inherited Compton from his uncle and namesake in 1596, having married Alice Molyneux. They had no children, and so on his death in 1608 the estate passed to his younger brother, Raleigh.

Raleigh Gilbert (d.1634)

The Popham colony in Maine

In April 1606 Sir Humphrey's youngest son, Raleigh, was granted a new royal licence to found two colonies in America. The first expedition, known as the London Colony, sailed from the capital, landing on the banks of the James River in May 1607, north of the lost colony of Roanoke. They named their settlement Jamestown in honour of the King, and, after numerous early difficulties, managed to establish it as the first permanent English colony in North America.

Raleigh Gilbert himself led the second, Plymouth Colony, with George Popham, the son of the Lord Chief Justice who had convicted Walter Raleigh of treason. They chose a more northern spot on the coast of Maine, where they built Fort St George, but Popham died during the bitter New England winter that followed. The next year Gilbert heard that his elder brother had also died and that he had inherited Compton Castle. He returned to Devon and travelled no more, but the seed from which modern America was to grow had at last been successfully planted.

The later Gilberts

The next two generations were content to live quietly at Compton. By the time of John Gilbert (1684–1733), the castle must have become difficult to live in, so he moved to Adrian Gilbert's old home at Sandridge. In 1785 his grandson, Edmund (1749-1816), sold Compton to James Templar of Stover and entered the church, becoming a vicar in Cornwall. Edmund's brother, Walter Raleigh Gilbert, joined the army, and, through his wife Nancy Hosken, they inherited Bodmin Priory, which became the principal family home through the 19th century. The next generation also chose between the church and the services, producing perhaps the most successful soldier in the family's history.

Lt-Gen. Sir Walter Raleigh Gilbert, 1st Bt (1785–1853)

Most of the Gilberts had looked west for adventure; Walter Raleigh Gilbert, by contrast, had a long career in India. In 1800, at the age of fifteen, he obtained a cadetship in the Bengal infantry. In 1803–4 he served with distinction in the battles of Delhi and Laswari and at the storming of Agra. During the First Anglo-Sikh War (1845–6) he commanded a division at the battles of Mudki, Ferozeshahr and Sobraon, winning high praise from his commanding officer: 'On this day his Division [was] enabled by his skill and courageous example to triumph over obstacles from which a less ardent spirit would have recoiled as insurmountable.' In the Second Anglo-Sikh War, he received the surrender of an entire army of 16,000 men and 41 guns at Rawalpindi. For his services he was created a baronet in 1851 and is commemorated by an obelisk on the Beacon at Bodmin.

Top Raleigh Gilbert

Above General Sir Walter Raleigh Gilbert in 1846

Opposite above Sir John Gilbert II

Opposite below Compton Castle in 1822, when it was a largely roofless ruin

23

Return and repair

The next three generations were all christened Walter Raleigh Gilbert, and again served either in the church or the armed forces.

In 1904, while training at Dartmouth for the Navy, the fifteen-year-old Walter Raleigh Gilbert (1889–1977) made a sentimental journey back to his old family home at Compton. Although the castle was by then almost derelict, he was determined one day to reclaim and restore it. That day finally arrived in 1931, when he succeeded in buying the ruins and the surrounding six acres. He began the slow process of clearing away the rampant ivy and restoring the castle to make it habitable for his wife Joan and their five children. Money was short, but he insisted on the right materials, building for generations to come.

In 1951 Commander Gilbert decided to hand over the castle and 300 acres of farmland to the National Trust on condition that he and his descendants could continue to live there. He rebuilt the collapsed Great Hall, which would provide a much-needed space for large social gatherings and give better access to the east and west wings, which, as the West Country historian A.L. Rowse remarked, 'were crying out to be reunited'. The work began in the summer of 1954 and was completed by 1956. Fortunately, they unearthed fragments of the Great Hall's original stone window mouldings built into nearby cottages that were due to be demolished. New, carefully matched stone came from the Hornton quarry in Oxfordshire. At the same time, the west wing was modernised to make comfortable living quarters for the family.

Commander Gilbert's son Geoffrey continues to live at Compton with his wife Angela and their three children, maintaining a proud link that goes back to the early 14th century and his namesake, the first Geoffrey Gilbert of Compton.

Above The Great Hall was rebuilt by Commander Gilbert

Bibliography

Coote, Stephen, *A Play of Passion: The Life of Sir Walter Ralegh*, 1993.
Everett, A.W., 'The Rebuilding of the Hall of Compton Castle', *Transactions of the Devonshire Association*, 1956, pp.75–85.
Haslam, Richard, 'Compton Castle', *Country Life*, 5 November 1981, pp.1546–50.
Martin, Paula, *Spanish Armada Prisoners: The Story of the Nuestra Señora del Rosario and her Crew* ... , Exeter Maritime Studies 1, 1988.
Milton, Giles, *Big Chief Elizabeth*, 2000.
Quinn, D.B., ed., 'The Voyages and Colonising Enterprises of Sir Humphrey Gilbert', 2 vols., *Hakluyt Society*, 2nd ser., 83–4, 1940.
Trevelyan, Raleigh, *Sir Walter Raleigh*, 2002.

Acknowledgements

This new guidebook draws heavily on the previous edition, which was largely written by Commander W.R. Gilbert. I am also indebted to Geoffrey and Angela Gilbert for their advice and hospitality.
Oliver Garnett

© 2005 The National Trust   Registered charity no.205846
ISBN 1-84359-149-9

Illustrations: British Museum, Dept. of Prints & Drawings pp.17 (right), 21 (bottom); English Heritage/National Monuments Record p.14; Geoffrey Gilbert p.3 (top);Hakluyt Society p.19; London Library p.15 (bottom); National Maritime Museum p.16; National Portrait Gallery, London pp.2 (left), 18, 21 (top), 23 (top and bottom); National Trust pp.19, 20, 22 (bottom); NT/David Garner p.9; NT/B. Kennedy-Bruyneels pp.3 bottom, 6, 7 (bottom), 8, 11 (top and bottom); National Trust Photographic Library back cover; NTPL/Christopher Hurst p.17 (left); NTPL/Ian Shaw front cover, pp.1, 2 (right), 4 (top and bottom left and right); NTPL/Francesco Venturi pp.5 (left and right), 7 (top), 10, 12, 13, 15 (top), 24.

Designed by Rose-Innes Associates

Print managed by Astron (HGP) for the National Trust (Enterprises) Ltd, 36 Queen Anne's Gate, London, SW1H 9AS